Postcards from Space

The Chris Hadfield Story

Postcards from Space

The Chris Hadfield Story

Story by Heather Down

Photo Credits: NASA
Postcard Credits: NASA (Photos taken by Colonel Chris Hadfield)

An imprint of
Wintertickle PRESS

Published by Echo Books, an imprint of Wintertickle Press
92 Caplan Avenue, Suite 155
Barrie, ON, Canada L4N 0Z7

winterticklepress.com
facebook.com/winterticklepress

Library and Archives Canada Cataloguing in Publication

Down, Heather, 1966-, author
Postcards from space : the Chris Hadfield story / story by Heather Down.

ISBN 978-1-894813-64-8 (pbk.).--ISBN 978-1-894813-68-6 (bound)

1. Hadfield, Chris--Juvenile literature. 2. Astronautics--Juvenile literature. 3. Astronauts--Canada--Biography--Juvenile literature. I. Title.

TL789.85.H33D69 2013 j629.450092 C2013-905109-0

NOTE: Wintertickle Press is an independent publishing company and is in no way associated with NASA or endorsed by NASA or Chris Hadfield. All photos in this book are credited to NASA whether marked so or not. For more information on NASA photography, please visit www.nasa.gov.

All "postcard" photos in this book were taken by Commander Chris Hadfield on the 34/35 International Space Station Mission. This resource is for information purposes only and validity of facts are not guaranteed by the author or Wintertickle Press.

Postcards from Space

The Chris Hadfield Story

For Logan and Brynleigh.
May the sky be your limit.

Some people say that Colonel Chris Hadfield is the coolest astronaut *ever*. He has walked in space. He has commanded the International Space Station and he has written postcards from space—well, not really, because that's just crazy! Have you ever seen a post office on the International Space Station? I didn't think so.

Commander Hadfield did the next best thing to sending postcards, though. He shared his trip with the world using social media. He sent notes, pictures, videos and songs all across the earth so everyone could feel like an astronaut too.

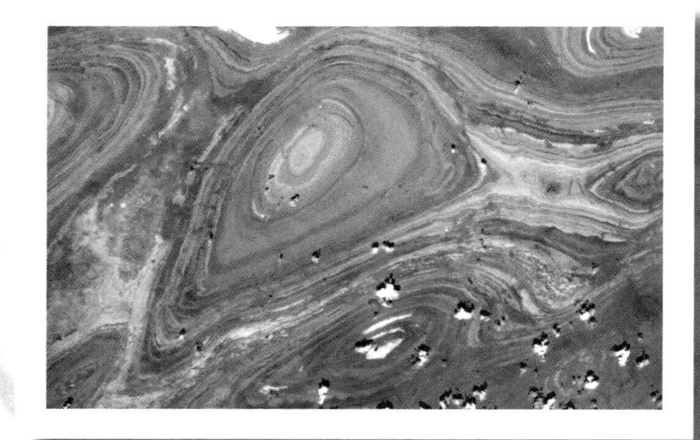

Neil Armstrong
Photo Credit: NASA

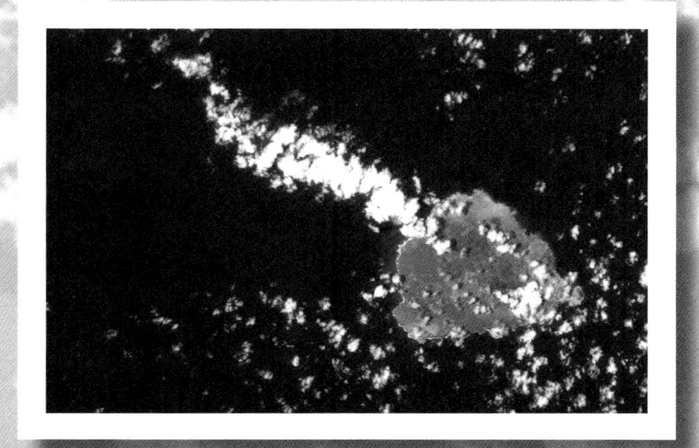

Chris wasn't always an astronaut. He was born in Sarnia and later moved to Milton, Ontario. Chris lived on a farm and learned all about working hard. When Chris was just nine years old he watched the Apollo moon landing on TV. He saw Neil Armstrong walk on the moon and Chris thought, "I'd like to be an astronaut one day."

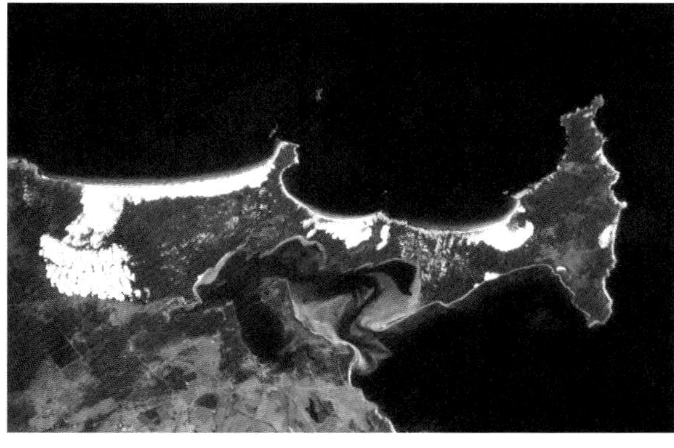

Chris knew that becoming an astronaut wouldn't be easy. He would have to work hard. That did not scare him or make him give up. He learned to fly gliders and airplanes. Eventually he became a test pilot. Even though Chris wanted to become an astronaut, he took time to do some other things he loved too—like playing guitar, singing, skiing, writing, running and playing volleyball.

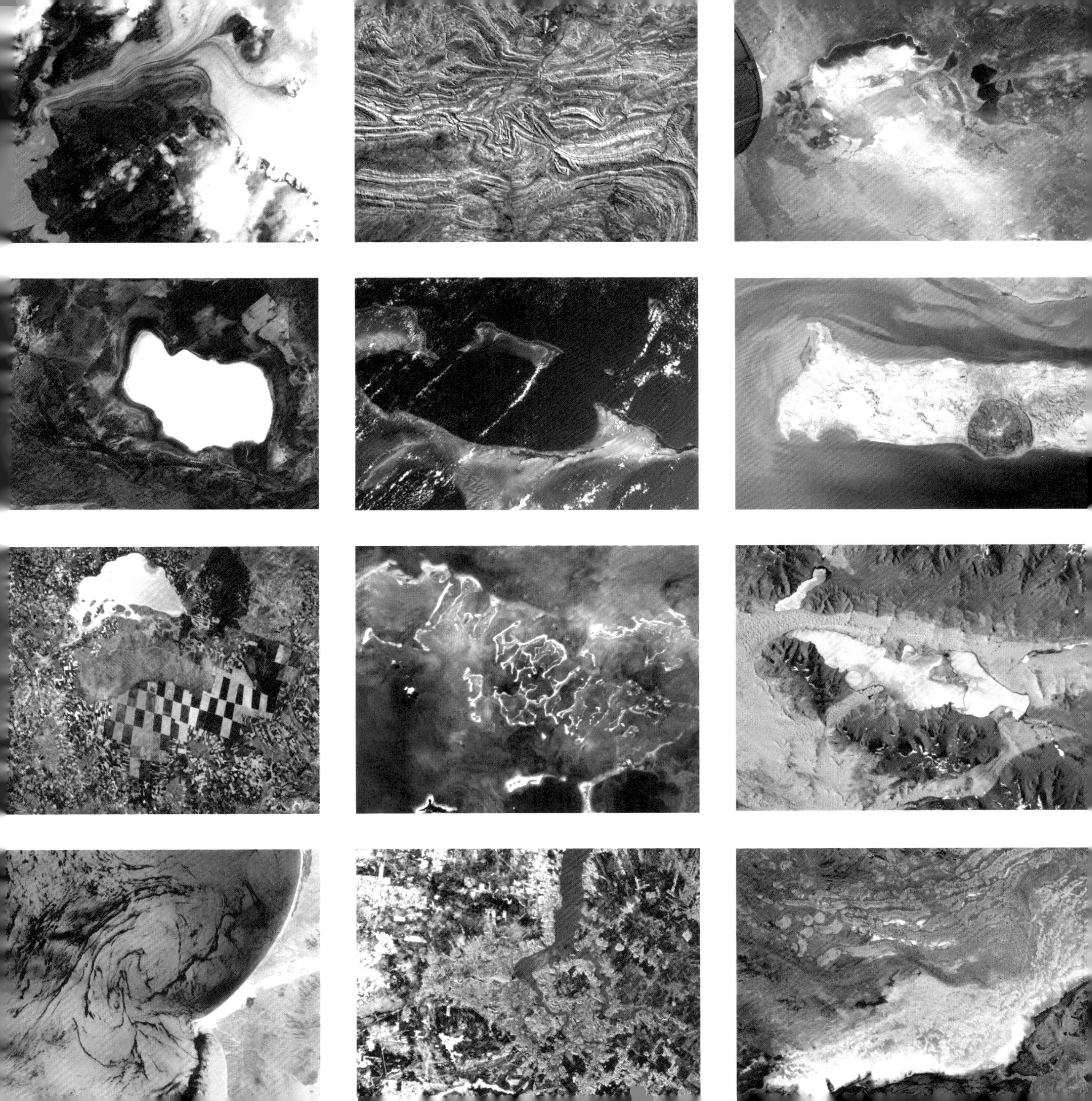

In 1992 Chris was chosen to become one of four new Canadian astronauts. He was one of 5,330 people who wanted to be an astronaut. That's a lot of people! But, he did not give up just because of that. He tried anyway. And, he was picked.

1995 Rocket Launch
Photo Credit: NASA

In 1995 Russia had a space station called Mir. Colonel Hadfield went on the second shuttle mission to Mir to take food, water and scientific supplies to the Russian cosmonauts who were living in space. He was the first Canadian to operate the Canadarm in orbit. The Canadarm is a robotic arm used to do repairs outside the station.

In 2001 Colonel Hadfield went into space again. This time he was on Space Shuttle Endeavour. He helped to deliver and install the Canadarm2 at the International Space Station. He performed two space walks. He was the first Canadian to ever leave a spacecraft and float freely in space.

ISS POWER TOOL

Chris Hadfield
Photo Credit: NASA

In 2012 Colonel Hadfield went on his third mission into space. He travelled up to the International Space Station. He was launched aboard the Russian Soyuz, a tiny spacecraft, to go live in space for five months. Partway through the mission on March 13, 2013, Chris became the first Canadian to command the International Space Station. He was now Commander Hadfield.

There were lots of things to get done at the International Space Station. Because there is no gravity in space, a lot of things have to be done differently. Everything from eating to sleeping to washing were not the same. Also, because there is no gravity to pull on an astronaut's bones and muscles, they can become weak. The astronaut has to exercise two hours every day just to try to stay strong!

Chris Hadfield
Photo Credit: NASA

There were experiments to conduct, pictures to take, and repairs and maintenance to do on the International Space Station. Even though he was so busy, Commander Hadfield still found time to do interviews with TV stations, send messages to the earth, answer questions, share beautiful pictures from space, create videos, and even sing!

Because the Space Station orbits the world in space, the astronauts on board have 16 sunrises and 16 sunsets all in one day! Wow. Imagine how confusing that could be.

On May 13, 2013, Colonel Hadfield came back to earth aboard the Soyuz spacecraft with Tom Marshburn and Roman Romanenko. They had to sit tightly in the craft for the trip back. They landed safely in Kazakhstan and had to be helped out of the shuttle. It felt very different to experience gravity for the first time after five months in space! Colonel Hadfield was excited to have a warm shower and eat regular food again.

Photo Credit: NASA

Chris Hadfield flew back to Houston, Texas, to the Johnson Space Center. He had to have lots of tests to see how being in space changed his body. He had to recover and do special exercises to get strong again and he had to get used to gravity. It was hard work but Chris still wasn't scared of hard work!

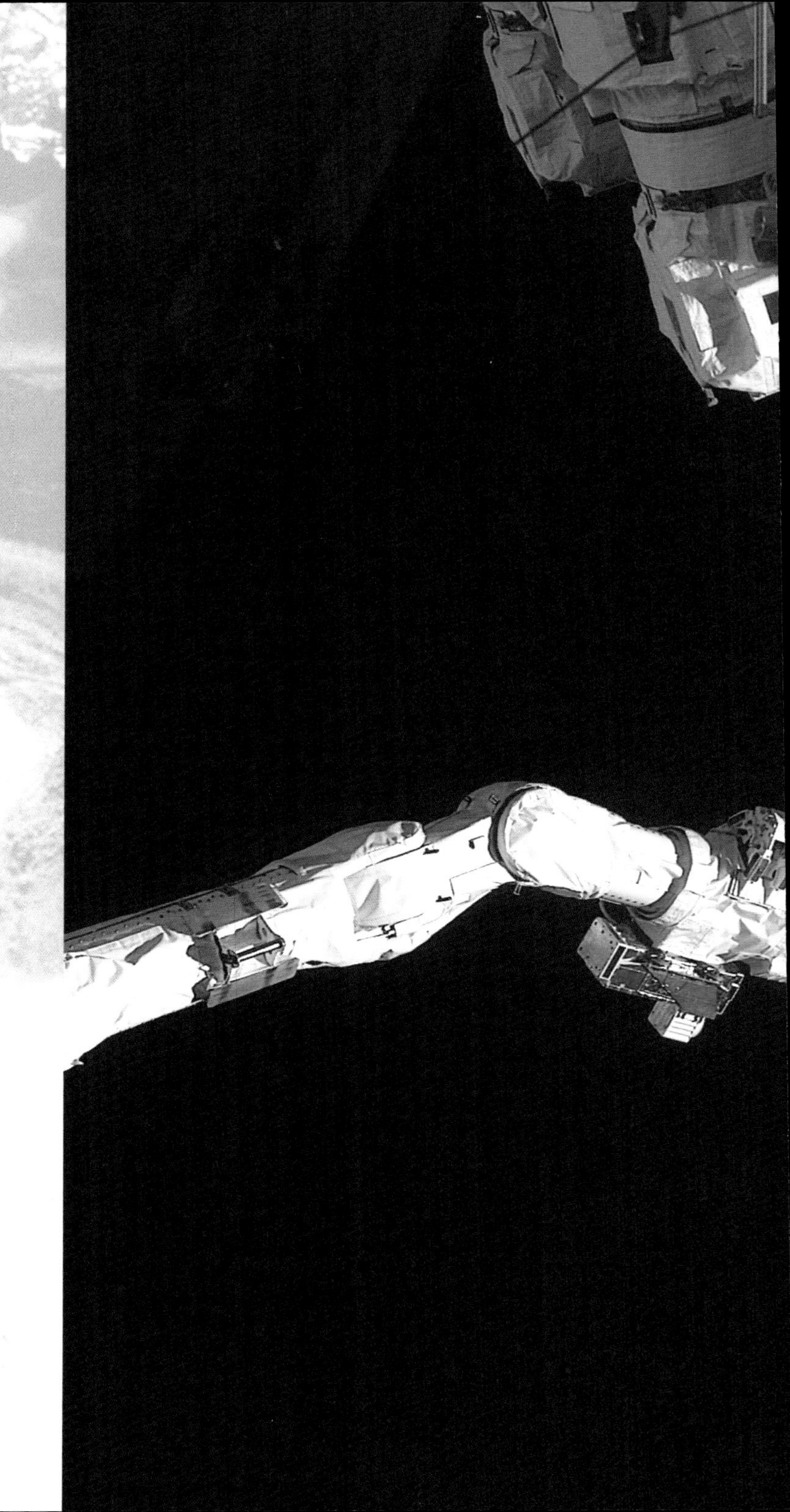

Photo Credit: NASA

Photo Credit: NASA

When Chris was a boy, he had an idea that he wanted to be an astronaut and explore space. Not everyone can become an astronaut. And, not everyone wants to be an astronaut. Maybe you want to be a dentist; or maybe a dog walker. Or maybe you want to be the dog walker's dentist. It doesn't matter what you want to be. If you really want to do something and work hard, it might just happen.

But remember, you will never be able to send postcards from space. *That's just crazy!*

Note:

While commanding the International Space Station, Canadian astronaut Chris Hadfield took thousands of breathtaking pictures of our planet. He was kind enough to share them with the world using social media. His "postcards" from space were spectacular and well-loved by thousands of followers. This book not only tells his story, but showcases some of his amazing photography. Thank you, Colonel Hadfield!

Hull and the Humber Estuary, U.K.

Paraguay

Big and Little Ambergris, Cay

Cayman Islands

Florida Keys, U.S.A.

Richat Structure, Mauritania

Outback, Australia

Ancient Saharan Stone, Algeria

Ascension Island

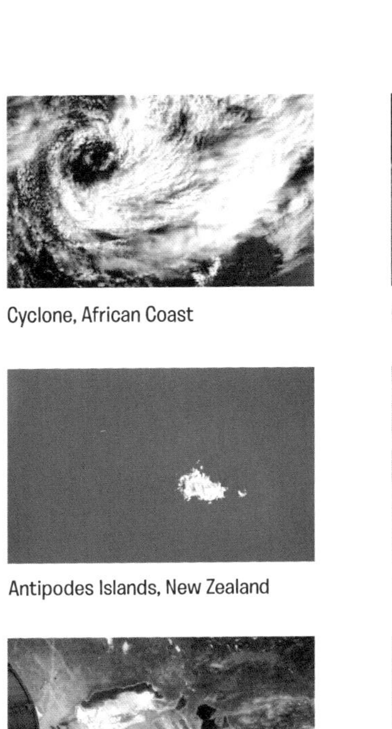

Cyclone, African Coast

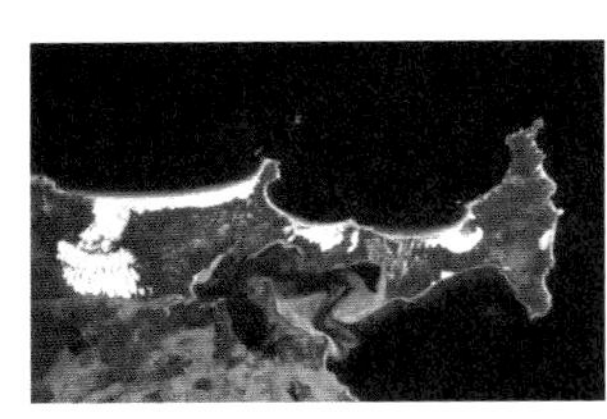

Coffin Bay, Australia.

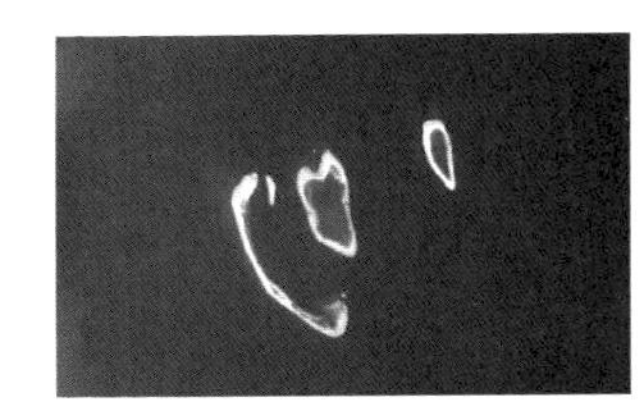

Great Barrier Reef, Australia

Antipodes Islands, New Zealand

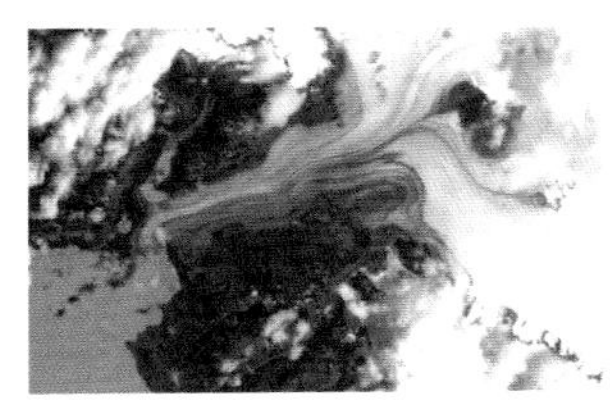

Viedma Glacier, Argentina

Outback, Australia

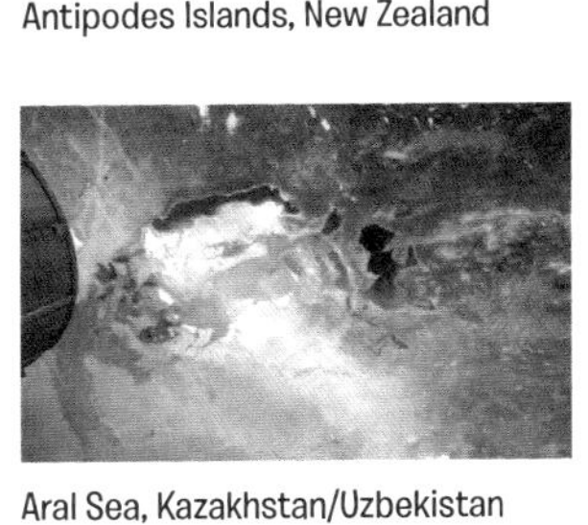

Aral Sea, Kazakhstan/Uzbekistan

Outback, Australia

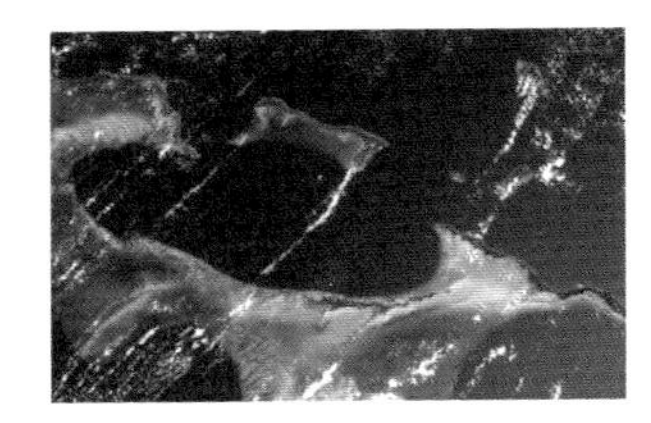

Bahamas

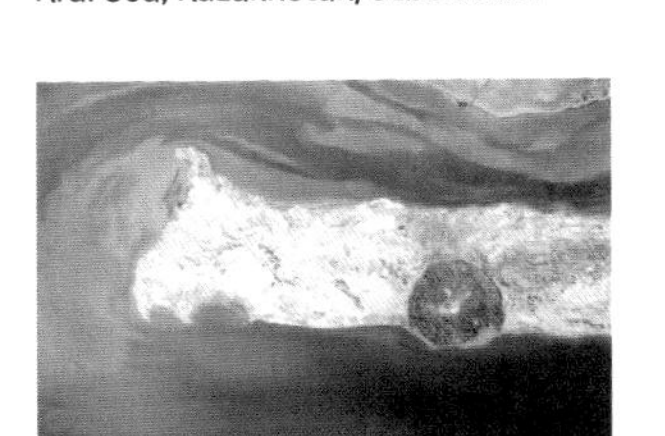

Straits of Hormuz, Qeshm island, Iran

Turkey

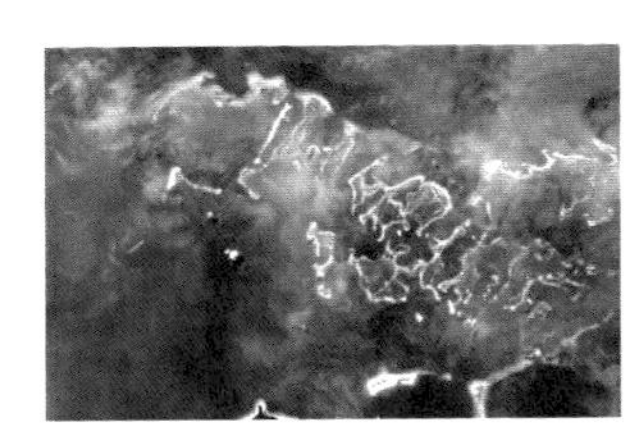

Coral Reef, Cuba

Highland, Mongolia

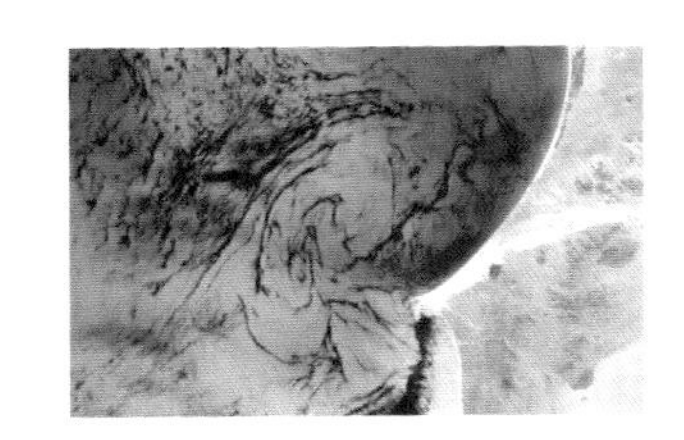

Sonora, Mexico

Bay of Fundy, Canada

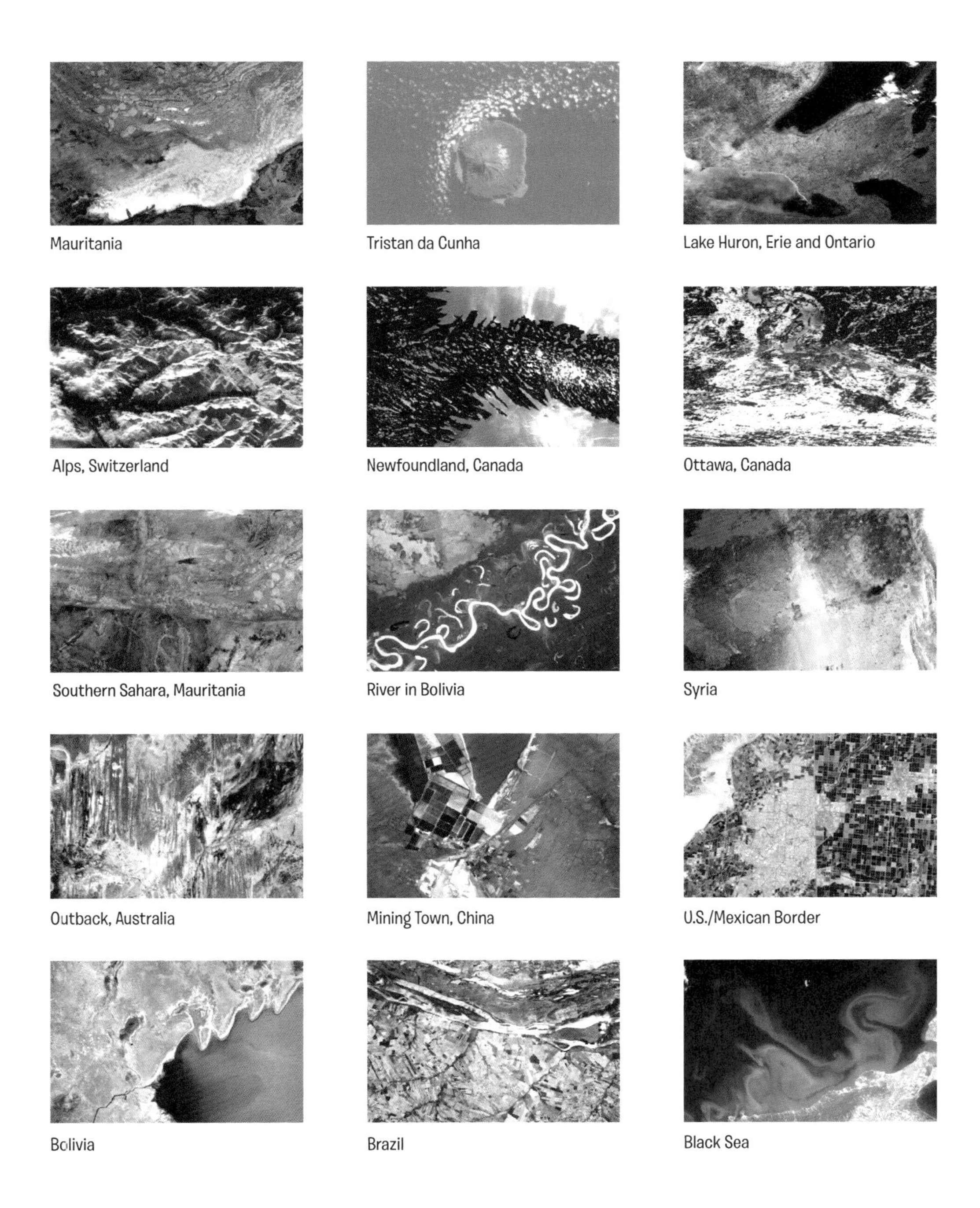

Mauritania

Tristan da Cunha

Lake Huron, Erie and Ontario

Alps, Switzerland

Newfoundland, Canada

Ottawa, Canada

Southern Sahara, Mauritania

River in Bolivia

Syria

Outback, Australia

Mining Town, China

U.S./Mexican Border

Bolivia

Brazil

Black Sea

East Coast, Africa

Moon

View of Horizon

Sunset on Horizon of Australia

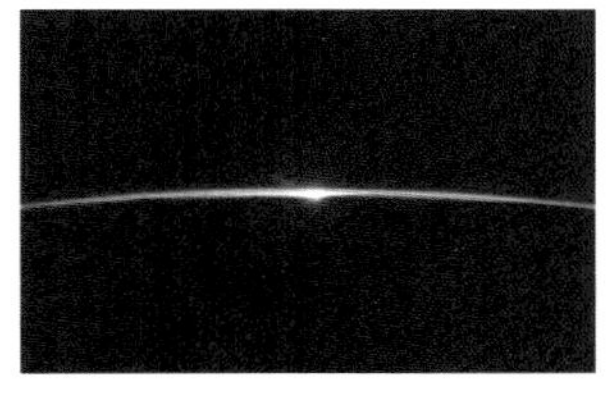

New Dawn

Amesbury, U.K.

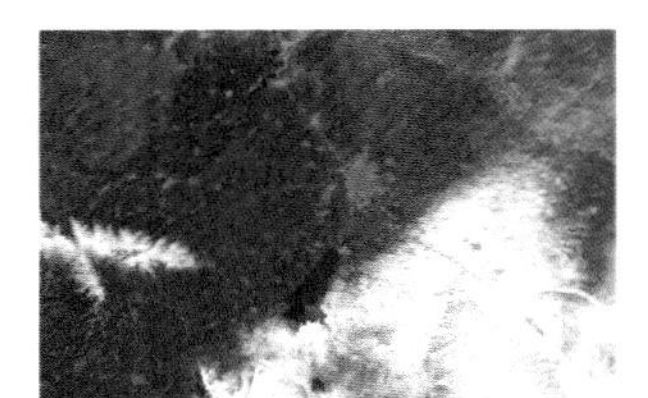

Homs, Syria

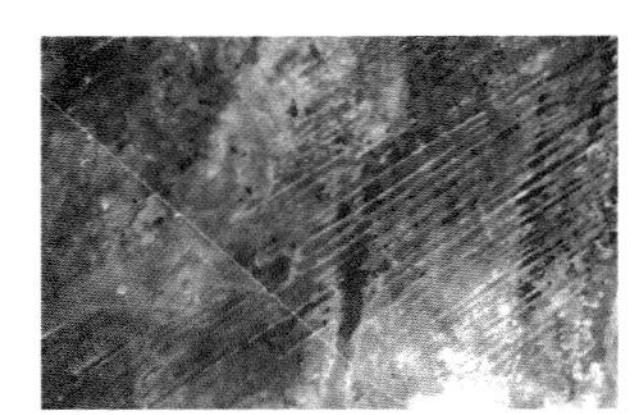

South Central Africa

About the Author:

Heather Down loves writing about all things Canadian. She has authored a novel for young adults called *A Deadly Distance* and a picture book called *Charity's Chirp,* illustrated by Jon Larter. In her spare time, Heather loves reading, writing, photography and running long distances.

Also available through Wintertickle Press:

Postcards from Space: The Chris Hadfield Story Activity Book
by Heather Down, ISBN 978-1-894813-65-5